There's No Place Like Space!

I'm the Cat in the Hat,
and we're off to have fun.
We'll visit the planets,
the stars, and the sun!

The Cat in the Hat's Learning Library™
introduces beginning readers to basic non-
fiction. If your child can read these lines,
then he or she can begin to understand the
fascinating world in which we live.

Learn to read. Read to learn.

This book comes from the home of

THE CAT IN THE HAT

RANDOM HOUSE, INC.

For a list of books in **The Cat in the Hat's**
Learning Library, *see the back endpaper.*

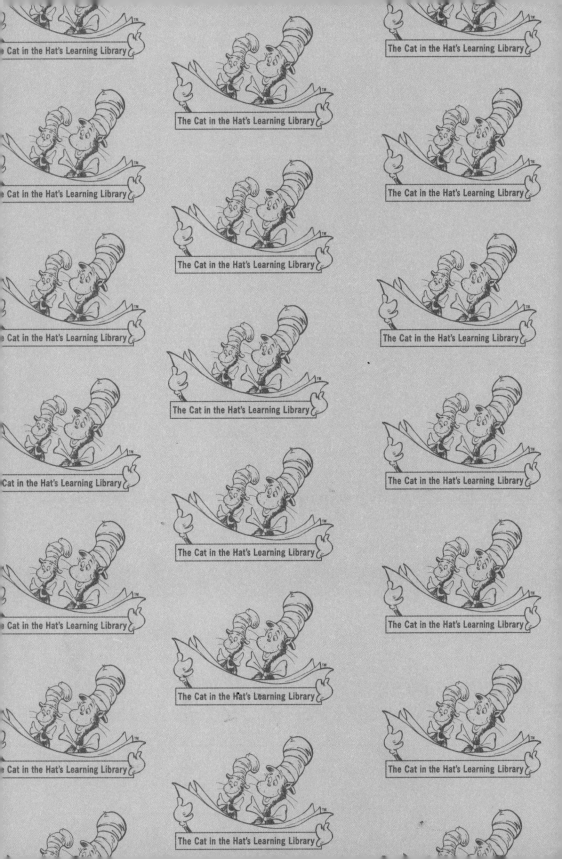

There's No Place
Like Space!

To John with love—T.R.

The editors would like to thank
BARBARA KIEFER, Ph.D.,
Associate Professor of Reading and Literature,
Teacher's College, Columbia University, and
AMIE GALLAGHER, Astronomy Educator,
the Hayden Planetarium at the American Museum of Natural History,
for their assistance in the preparation of this book.

www.randomhouse.com/kids

Library of Congress Cataloging-in-Publication Data
Rabe, Tish.
There's no place like space / by Tish Rabe.
    p.   cm. — (The Cat in the Hat's learning library)
SUMMARY: Dr. Seuss's Cat in the Hat introduces Sally and Dick to the planets,
stars, and moons in our universe.
ISBN 0-679-89115-3 (trade). — ISBN 0-679-99115-8 (lib. bdg.)
1. Astronomy—Juvenile literature. [1. Astronomy.] I. Title. II. Series.
QB46.R28   1999   520—dc21   97-52315

Printed in the United States of America   October 1999   10 9 8 7 6 5 4 3 2 1

There's No Place Like Space!

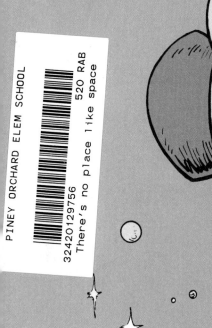

by Tish Rabe

illustrated by Aristides Ruiz

The Cat in the Hat's Learning Library™

Random House 🏠 New York

I'm the Cat in the Hat,
and we're off to have fun.
We'll visit the planets,
the stars, and the sun!

There is no place like space.

I will prove it to you.

Your mother will
not mind at all if I do.

Jump in! Here we go!
We will fly up so high
we can dance on the moon
and play games in the sky.

We will swing past the stars,
and in case you have missed 'em,
you'll soon see...

the planets
in our solar system!

There are nine of these planets
that circle the sun,
and soon you'll be able
to name every one.

Mercury's
close to the sun's burning light.
It is hot in the daytime...
but freezing at night.

On Venus the weather
is always the same—
hot, dry, and windy,
with no chance of rain.

TODAY's WEATHER ON VENUS: REALLY, REALLY HOT! NEARLY 900° FAHRENHEIT! WINDY and DRY

Can you guess the next planet?
Well, here is a clue:
It is my home and home
to Thing One and Thing Two.

You have been living on it
each day since your birth.
It is third from the sun—
it is **our** planet...

...Earth!
It spins all the time,
round and round like a top.
It turns once every day
and it never will stop.

HOME
SWEET
HOME

This question had Thing One and
Thing Two in a tizzy:

If the Earth's always spinning,
why don't we feel dizzy?

We don't feel the Earth
as it spins on its way
'cause we're spinning right with it
right now every day.

Next, here is Mars.
It's the color of rust.
We sneeze here because
it is covered with dust.

Travel to Jupiter
and you will find
it is bigger than all
other planets combined.

Saturn has rings.
It's so light—
who would think?

It could float in an ocean
and not even sink!

A planet can have
satellites that surround it.
Uranus has lots of these
objects around it.

There are colors in space.

I will show some to you.

Neptune, you see,

is a beautiful blue.

If you lived on Pluto,
it would not be nice.
Some astronomers think
it is covered with ice.

It is chilly and cold
every night and all day,
for the sun's just a speck
in the sky far away.

26

An astronomer studies
what's up in the sky.
Thing Two wants to be one.
In fact, so do I!

27

We have seen all nine planets.
Now here is a trick
to remember their names
and remember them quick.

Say:

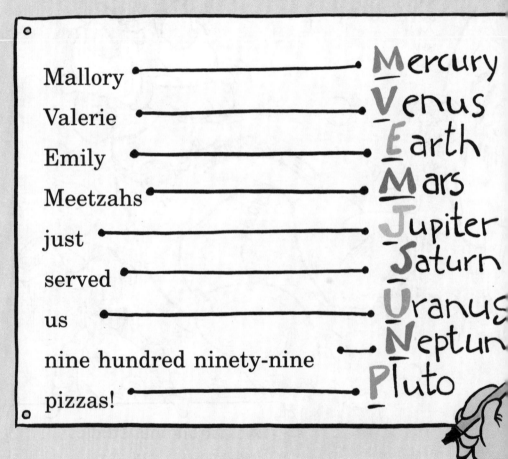

Mallory	**M**ercury
Valerie	**V**enus
Emily	**E**arth
Meetzahs	**M**ars
just	**J**upiter
served	**S**aturn
us	**U**ranus
nine hundred ninety-nine	**N**eptune
pizzas!	**P**luto

The first letter of each of these words is the same as the first letter in each of the planets you name.

Now here is a game
you can play in the skies:
Connect all the stars
you can see with your eyes.

GREAT DOG

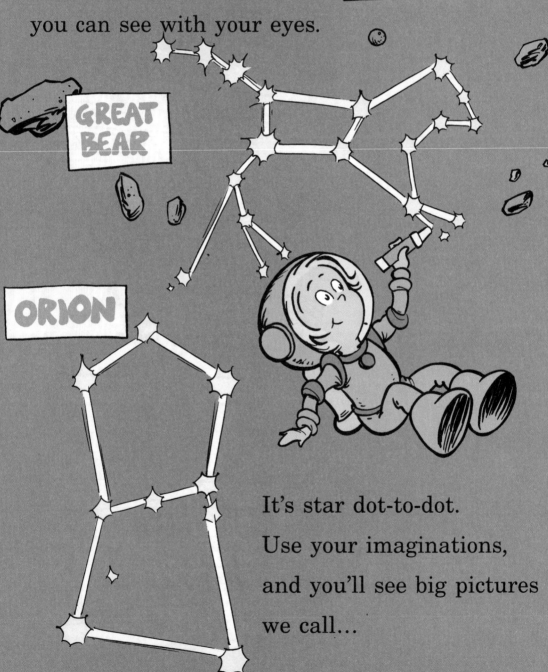

GREAT BEAR

ORION

It's star dot-to-dot.
Use your imaginations,
and you'll see big pictures
we call...

...constellations!

The Bull

LION

A dog, the Great Bear,
and Leo the Lion,
Taurus the Bull,
and a hunter—Orion!

A star in the sky
may look small, like a dot,
but it's really a big, glowing ball,
and it's **hot**.

And there's one star by far
that's our favorite one.
We can't live without it:
the star called...

...the sun!

From the Earth, it looks big.
There is one reason why.
It's the closest to Earth
of the stars in the sky.

But be careful and
never look right at the sun.
Your eyes would get hurt,
and that would not be fun.

How big is the sun?
We just heard
right this minute
a million of our Earths
could all fit right in it.

Oh, look at the time!
We must go very soon.
But first we must take
a quick look at the moon.

The moon does not shine
in the sky in the night
but, like a big mirror,
reflects the sun's light.

37

The universe is
a mysterious place.
We are only just learning
what happens in space.

So I brought you a present!
To look in the sky—
just put this telescope
up to your eye.

Oh dear, I must go
fly back up to the stars
and take Things One and Two
out to dinner on Mars.

But there's lots to discover,
and it might be you
who looks up in the sky...

and finds something
that's new!

GLOSSARY

Astronomer: A person who studies the planets, stars, sun, moon, and other heavenly bodies.

Constellation: A group of stars that form a pattern in the sky that looks like a picture.

Satellite: A natural or man-made object that moves around a planet.

Solar system: The sun and all the planets that move around it.

Telescope: An instrument that uses lenses to make faraway objects appear closer.

Universe: Everything that exists, including the earth, the planets, the stars, and all of space.

FOR FURTHER READING

Astronauts Today by Rosanna Hansen (Random House, *Picturebacks*®). An introduction to space flight, illustrated with NASA photographs. For preschoolers and up.

The Big Dipper by Franklyn M. Branley, illustrated by Molly Coxe (HarperTrophy, *Let's-Read-and-Find-Out Science*®, Stage 1). All about the Big Dipper, the Little Dipper, and the North Star. For preschoolers and up.

The Earth and Sky by Gallimard Jeunesse and Jean-Pierre Verdet, illustrated by Sylvaine Perols (Scholastic, *A First Discovery Book*). A look at the Earth from above and below its surface. For preschoolers and up.

Is There Life in Outer Space? by Franklyn M. Branley, illustrated by Don Madden (HarperTrophy, *Let's-Read-and-Find-Out Science*®, Stage 2). A funny but serious introduction to the concept of life on other planets. For grades 1 and up.

INDEX

The Cat in the Hat's Learning Library

The Cat in the Hat's Learning Library

The Cat in the Hat's Learning Library

The Cat in the Hat's Learning Library

The Cat in the Hat's Learning Library

The Cat in the Hat's Learning Library

The Cat in the Hat's Learning Library

The Cat in the Hat's Learning Library

The Cat in the Hat's Learning Library

The Cat in the Hat's Learning Library

The Cat in the Hat's Learning Library

The Cat in the Hat's Learning Library

The Cat in the Hat's Learning Library

The Cat in the Hat's Learning Library

The Cat in the Hat's Learning Library

The Cat in the Hat's Learning Library

The Cat in the Hat's Learning Library

The Cat in the Hat's Learning Library

The Cat in the Hat's Learning Library

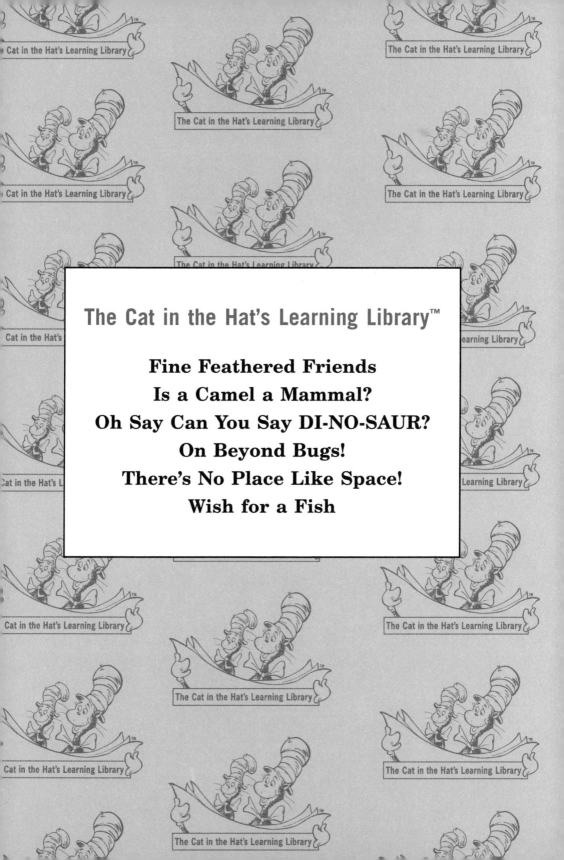

The Cat in the Hat's Learning Library™

Fine Feathered Friends
Is a Camel a Mammal?
Oh Say Can You Say DI-NO-SAUR?
On Beyond Bugs!
There's No Place Like Space!
Wish for a Fish